HEAVENLY
POETRY
OF PROPHECY

HEAVENLY
POETRY
OF PROPHECY

poems and prophetic activations
from the tree of life
free of strife

Veronica McDonald

RAVENSOUND
PUBLISHING

Author email: contact@veronicamcdonald.com.au

Ravensound Publishing
Brisbane, QLD, Australia

Editor: Justine Talbot
Cover and Typesetting: David Tensen

Heavenly Poetry of Prophecy / Veronica McDonald

ISBN 978-0-9875345-4-5

PREFACE

*"Come sit at the table with Me
and you will see."*

-Jesus

DEDICATION

I dedicate Heavenly Poetry of Prophecy to
my children,
Hannah, Nathan, David, Stephen
and Joshua,
whose love and light is the joy of my life!

INTRODUCTION

This book was birthed out of a dream. In this dream, I opened my front door and saw an entire tree nursery had been given to me. I noticed trees in transplant bags; they had been uprooted. Some had deep roots, whilst others had some new shoots. All were in protective bags. There was much variety – different ages, stages, shapes - all ready to be established and not die!

The purpose of this book is to bring you into encounter with the tree of life, free of strife! To establish you. One kiss with the King that changes everything! To bring you into a well-watered space, where you can get established with roots that go deep; your branches providing rest and shade for others to come and meet. Deep rest, free from the hamster wheel of strife.

Calvary has the last say! Man's religion, tradition, culture and self-effort; the tree of good and evil - Jesus bore it all, so you could have it all! Heaven came to Earth so you could give birth!

My prayer is that Holy Spirit will touch your heart and mind with the mind of Christ in you, as you find joy in embracing the truth through the supernatural life of grace. It's time to fly; the revelation of rest releasing you from the sty! The Gospel is simple, yet not simplistic! It's the power you need to thrive in life!

You are dignified! You are worthy! You walk in light! You're a beautiful butterfly, one whose frequency releases light! It's time to arise! Peace poet, these activations are yours for the taking! They precede all that is yours,

"You are Heaven's delight!"

Much love,

Veronica. X

Genesis 3:22-23 The Passion Translation

The Tree of Life Must be Planted in the soil of the Human Heart

And Yahweh-God said,

"The man has become like one of us, knowing good and evil, and now he might take in his hands from the Tree of Life, and eat it, and live forever."

Therefore, Yahweh-God expelled him from Eden's paradise to till the ground from which he was taken.

(Taken from the earth, he now is given the earth to till. Turning over the soil is a picture of how man must guard his heart, his life. We must become those who have been loosened and opened to the rain of God. The Tree of Life must be planted

in the soil of the human heart.)

TABLE OF CONTENTS

PREFACE V

DEDICATION VI

INTRODUCTION VII

LOVE ISN'T RUNNING OUT ON YOU....................... 1

THE TAP OF FAITHFULNESS IN YOU 2

HOT PURSUIT... 3

HOPE ALIVE, DREAMS BURSTING TO LIFE........... 4

MERCY'S KISS 5

OUT OF THE BIND
NO LONGER BLIND 6

PATIENT IN LOVE 7

YOU ARE ON HIS MIND 8

RULE AND REIGN 9

DEATH, WHERE'S YOUR STING?............................ 10

DEATH TO LIFE.. 11

THE REAL DEAL... 12

SOAR ON HIS ROAR... 13

FAITH IS HERE,
GRACE IS NEAR... 14

LASER FOCUS ON YOU 15

THE GATE 16

TRUST IS A MUST 17

PROMOTION AMID PROCESS 18

BLOODIED AND BRUISED 19

BROKEN SHALL GO 20

NEW IS UPON YOU 21

MOMENTUM BLOCKERS NO LONGER
STOPPERS 22

THIS BATTLE IS WON 23

PERMISSION GRANTED 24

WISDOM CALLS 25

CYCLES OF DEFEAT UNDER YOUR FEET 26

AMAZING GRACE 27

YOU'VE COME FAR 28

FAVOUR IS YOUR SHIELD 29

THIS TOO SHALL PASS 30

SEEN IN THE LEAN AND IN-BETWEEN 31

ALL THINGS NEW 32

BREAKTHROUGH
UPON YOU 33

IMPERFECT ACTION BETTER THAN NO ACTION ... 34

MIS-GUIDED ONES ARE COMING THROUGH...... 35

YOU'RE NOT LATE... 36

THE MESSAGE REMAINS, THE
METHODS CHANGE... 37

THE WEDDING AND THE WINE 38

MESSY IS BEAUTIFUL.. 39

FAITH AND PATIENCE 40

STAY IN YOUR LANE.. 41

FAITHFULNESS SEES 42

REST BRINGING YOU GODS BEST 43

CROWNED AND COMMISSIONED 44

VICTORY IS HEAVEN'S DECREE.............................. 45

SOAR ON HEAVEN'S ROAR 46

THE HUSTLE 47

YOU'RE GOING TO FLY 48

NEW CEILINGS, NEW FLOORS................................. 49

DREAMS ARE BURSTING TO LIFE 50

PROMISE OF PROMOTION 51

REFRESHING RAIN IS HERE 52

MIRACLE TIME.. 53

NO MORE STARK 54

HOLD THE LINE... 55

NEW SHOES 56

TWO TREES 58

ANOTHER OPPORTUNITY 60

NO MORE LOOSE CHANGE...................................... 61

WOUNDED AND WEARY 62

ALL THINGS NEW 63

HE NAILED IT FOR YOU AND FOR ME 64

NOT FORGOTTEN.. 66

YOU ARE MY DELIGHT.. 67

VICTORY IS IN SIGHT.. 68

PIT TO PALACE 69

ANCHORED TO HOPE.. 70

NOT GOING DOWN 71

A PAUSE IS POWERFUL.. 72

RAINBOW OF PROMISE 74

PIONEERS, YOU ARE DEAR 75

HEAVEN'S HONEY 76

TRUST IS A MUST.. 77

THE BEST IS YET TO COME 78

LOVE HAS WON 79

LOVE ISN'T RUNNING OUT
ON YOU

Sealed, it's a deal!
The Father and Son cut an everlasting seal for you!
Dry, barren places shall not have the best of you!
Complete order and spiritual perfection upon you!
Laser focus; centred;
Love is never running out on you!

THE TAP OF FAITHFULNESS
IN YOU

Sarah laughed, she tapped in, too!
Faithfulness upon you!
You're going to tap into faithfulness
and experience miraculous breakthrough, too!
Faith has positioned you!

HOT PURSUIT

All things new upon you!
Your heart - your dreams, are coming through!
Love in pursuit of you!
Dare to believe, you're pressing through!
Love's hot pursuit for you!

HOPE ALIVE, DREAMS
BURSTING TO LIFE

Destiny lives in you!
Healing isn't based on your faith;
It's based on Heaven's love poured out for you!
A perspective shift is leading you forth - swift!
Breakthrough!
All things new, healing upon you!
It's time to start drinking,
Out of the cerebral mind,
Into the mind of Christ in you!
Hope alive!
Dreams are bursting to life!

MERCY'S KISS

Faith has positioned you!
Breakthrough; 2 by 2, you're coming through!
Upgrade! Increase!
Mercy's kiss amid the dis!
Bliss!
The Father and Son cut a covenant for you!
Heaven qualifies you to tap in!
2 by 2, you're breaking through!

OUT OF THE BIND
NO LONGER BLIND

The hamster wheel performance no longer in your
hand;
You're accepted and free!
Received! Released!
Religion has lost its hold on you!
You are a find!
Out of the bind, no longer blind!

PATIENT IN LOVE

Patience is madly in love with you!
Not anxious about you; not taken by surprise;
You are His prize!
Patience says, "My faithfulness shall follow you
all the days of your life - it's true!
When the world puts you in spin,
I AM your breakthrough!
Amid the pressure you're facing today,
listen to what I have to say:
"Rest in My perfect test!"

YOU ARE ON HIS MIND

You're on Heaven's mind,
And you're on time!
He has the dime!
You've done all you can do,
Now it's time to hand it over and experience truce!
Breakthrough; miracles of provision;
Favour amid rejection;
God's best coming through for you!
You are on His mind;
He's lining things up for you!

RULE AND REIGN

The Man acquainted with sorrow has faced your
tomorrow!
Perspective shift, rule and reign, you're called to
service! Your future is in His hand;
He has the timespan in the land.
Rule and reign; provision is in the vision;
He's calling you up to face the calling for tomorrow!

DEATH, WHERE'S YOUR STING?

Death, where is your sting?
You walk with the resurrected King!
Broken trust, broken dreams that seem like dust!
Resurrection power is upon you in this hour!
Zacchaeus was willing to go!
Generous!
One kiss that caused him to release his grip!
He has a burden for tomorrow and a fresh start,
as one kiss changed his heart!
You're going to experience your fresh start!

DEATH TO LIFE

Today, Heaven's offering you peace!
Peace with God; peace with man!
Peace in your inner man.
Mercy and grace are drawing you home.
He doesn't want your money;
it all belongs to Him anyway.
He wants your heart connected to His.
Peace in your inner man!
He's the Lamb slain,
for all your suffering;
all your pain.
Sceptics who had it all:
Influence in the four walls of the Church;
man's religion - death has dealt with it all so you can
fly!
The carnal mind; the unpredictable; the irrational;
the behaviour that led to death;
He bled so you can rise!
We were dead in sin, now alive!

THE REAL DEAL

Fake versus true;
You're going to see the real amid the zoo;
The counterfeit no longer having a hold on you!
Passion, power, experience, breakthrough!
Religious tradition, culture and man
shall no longer hold you in the span!
The real is true!
All things new!
Out of the cerebral, into
the mind of Christ breaking you through!
The eternal realm in, upon and released through
you!

SOAR ON HIS ROAR

Standing on Heaven's roar,
It's time for more!
How you thought it would happen;
How you thought it would work out,
has been a set up for more!
They perceived Jesus was going to
fully establish God's kingdom in Jerusalem,
Yet he had to die;
The cup of suffering, before he could rise!
It's time for more!
Resurrection power is knocking on your door!
You've dreamed the dream;
You've birthed the dream;
The Lord has grown the dream,
but you feel unseen.
Others have dropped off and you feel loss.
In the in-between, lean.
God has so much in store,
It's time to soar on His roar.
You're going to let go of what has come and what
was done. Simply come.
Heaven's inviting you into more:
More power; more love; more presence amid the
stew!
Fresh peace!
New beginnings and fresh dew upon you!

FAITH IS HERE,
GRACE IS NEAR

What God has in store for you is way more!
Way more than you have imagined, dreamed or
asked.
Faith in action is upon you!
A doing word.
A verb.
It's tested and it's rested and the plan ahead is yet to
come! Faith is here; grace is near; you are dear!
No more delay - that thorn son;
That situation that keeps you from having fun,
Perfect love has defeated that sucker, son!
You're going to get your fresh run!

LASER FOCUS ON YOU

He's dealing with the feeling of diluted, distracted;
You're not on the road to nowhere!
Laser focus is upon you!
The sound of Heaven is with you;
You're not alone.
A magnet of the presence and power of the sword,
Faithful and true with you!
Suddenly, there's a shift
– Trauma; therapy;
Release from complexities and stresses unseen;
Fresh heat; laser focus has won!
Love has come!
You've won!

THE GATE

Timeless and true,
Eternity has broken through - for you!
The gate keeper knows you!
His promises are timeless and true, for YOU.
His voice is leading you.
Protecting you.
The safest place to be,
"You are found in Me," says the King of Glory.

TRUST IS A MUST

Trust is connected to your emotions
and Heaven is breaking through.
Jesus wept; He sees you!
Your nervous system is coming into alignment;
Fresh dew upon you.
Trust is your key in this hour, it's what's going to
thrust!
Divine connections with man, amid life's sty!
The dogs of destiny have had a chew!
The pious have not had the best of you!
The high mind that held you cannot keep you
as you encounter trust - it's a must!
You are safe here;
Heaven is breaking through.
You're going to retrieve, see reprieve and fly –
not die!

PROMOTION AMID PROCESS

Expect breakthrough!
Acceleration, fast!
Easy at last!
You're breaking free to higher ground!
Walls are coming down!
Where you've seen muzzle and guzzle and trouble,
You're going to see double!
Bloodied and bruised,
He too was abused!
Heaven relates to you!

Romans 10:1 TPT
"And how can the message be proclaimed if messengers have yet
to be sent? That's why the Scriptures say: How welcome is the
arrival of those proclaiming the joyful news of peace and of good
things to come!"

BLOODIED AND BRUISED

Bloodied, bruised feet - Heaven's giving you fresh
shoes! You've won and it's time to run with the
good news!
"You are heard; you are seen!
You're a part of My herd!"
Honour creates an atmosphere
for the presence of the Eternal to descend.
The rainbow of promise surrounds you.
Bloodied and bruised, your feet carry good news!
With peace you shall conquer and experience
breakthrough!

BROKEN SHALL GO

Disappointed, disillusioned, doubt shall go!
No more dope - you shall experience hope!
Delay is broken off you this day!
Promotion amid process you shall know!
Miracle magnet - the broken shall flow!

NEW IS UPON YOU

Time is on your side;
Holiness is your position - do you know?
A declaration of the truth shall slew!
Heaven's rain upon you!
Dew upon you!
The power of love breaking through!
Heaven's wind blowing upon you!
Refreshing rain, releasing you from pain.
Sexual addiction you shall no longer know.
You're going to flow!
Holiness is your position
and with holiness, you shall go!

MOMENTUM BLOCKERS NO
LONGER STOPPERS

The atmosphere of change is here.
The ministry of condemnation no longer here.
Chaos surrounds, but you are found!
One in the Son;
Won.
It's time to come!
Momentum blockers - no longer stoppers.
"Leave them to Me."
Come and fly free!

THIS BATTLE IS WON

Your heart is one!
Heaven is incomplete without you, son!
That's the invitation, "Simply Come!"
The Gospel is simple, not simplistic!
He's got you; you can come!
Leave behind the dung - it's done!

PERMISSION GRANTED

Jesus qualifies you, son!
Not your marital status;
Not your years of servitude;
Not your social status.
Not your bank balance, investment portfolio,
pedigree or actions!
HE qualifies you, and that's enough!
Permission Granted!
Enough!

WISDOM CALLS

What He's called you for, He will provide for!
Wisdom calls!
Come up higher and fly!
No longer held in a sigh!
You're going to say good-bye to the familiar and
stand tall! He bore it all, so you could receive it all!
You're worth it, amid the fall!

CYCLES OF DEFEAT UNDER
YOUR FEET

You're not a clown –
This circus isn't yours to perform in;
It's leaving your town!
Enter in and receive Heaven's best!
Peace that surpasses understanding and a new way
forward! Lack behind your back;
Tradition and culture no longer holding you back!
Perspective shift; you're stepping into more!
Cycles of defeat are under your feet;
The favour of God is with you in the sword!

AMAZING GRACE

Grace, your soft landing has sworn!
The covenant the Father and Son says, "It's done,
come!
Look how far you've come!"
Line in the sand;
He's taken you by the hand!
The bliss of mercy's kiss!
Faithful and true with you.
Soft landing amid the fall!
Tight rope of failure no more!
Prolonged situations and circumstances
that don't seem to fall;
Centred and true amazing grace is with you!
Laser focus on you!
Heavens' assignment and divine alignment,
Acceleration yours, because He has sworn!
Heaven on Earth;
Amazing grace, you're known!

YOU'VE COME FAR

How far you've come!
You're going to see there's a pause in the Son!
As you pause in His presence, you'll get more done!
The rest of God is an adjective;
It's receiving His power to get the job done!
Amazing grace, look how far you've come!
The pause is going to release you from strife.
Amazing grace with you!
Liberty, truth!
A yielded life will do!

FAVOUR IS YOUR SHIELD

Favour is with you!
Favour follows you!
Favour surrounds you!
Favour amid rejection - this too shall pass;
Favour shields you!
With favour you'll see provision, power and
breakthrough! Favour is with you!

THIS TOO SHALL PASS

In-dwelling presence sustains you!
The strength and stay of Heaven's kiss making way!
Line in the sand, you're going to see miracles in
your hand! Upgrade is here! This day!
The strength of an ox upon you, in the way.
Provision, protection, promise
as you pass through this dark tunnel along the way.

SEEN IN THE LEAN AND IN-BETWEEN

The Lord is my shepherd, I shall not want.
He sees me in the lean and in-between;
He gives me peace; I am seen.
Doors are opening on the run!
New places, new faces,
Triple 4, my ceiling becomes the floor!

John 4:44 TPT
"Now Jesus knew that prophets are honoured everywhere they go
except in their hometown."

ALL THINGS NEW

No more small - it's time to stand tall!
Your voice releases the sound!
Flourishing in the tree that was cut down!
The One who rose up from the ground!
Found!
Resurrection power in your town!
Vision, valley, victory!
Unbelievers, believers and sceptics in the crowd!
He wants your heart from the start!
The process of discovering truth shall uncover
acceptance
and the sceptic shall see clearly now!
All things new;
Fresh dew upon your loved ones, too!

BREAKTHROUGH

UPON YOU

Deliverance is upon you!
Fortitude is upon you!
It's the power of God bringing you through!
The wind of change is here!
Declare, decree;
The atmosphere of Heaven is bringing rain!
Recompense, restore and more!
You're going to experience release and soar!
Courage and kind leading you forth!
Remnant - you're not blind, weak, distorted or
diluted; TRUTH is with you!
Remnant, you're on the tip of the arrow breaking
through!

IMPERFECT ACTION BETTER
THAN NO ACTION

The loaves and the fishes are upon you!
Your YES is Heaven's best!
The 5%, the 10% - your seed, Heaven blows!
"Bring your offering to Me and watch and see!
Increase, abundance, seed time and harvest - it
belongs to Me. The wind and the water I command -
can you see?
Imperfect action pleases me." Says the King of
Glory. Perfection isn't the standard, can you see?
Bring your offering, your time, your talent, your
seed
and watch it explode as the breath of God blows!

MIS-GUIDED ONES ARE
COMING THROUGH

The enemy has a sniper view;
The eternal one has a peripheral view!
He's above, around and coming through!
Falsely accused, Love sees you!
The shame, the blame,
disappointment and exhaustion shall flee!
The mis-guided shall see through your decree!
Disarming and free, victory has come!
"Destiny shall be fulfilled in Me," says the King of
Glory. Centred and true, you're coming through;
The sniper shall not take you out!
Heaven's shield protects you!

YOU'RE NOT LATE

Ambassador of the highest government, that's you!
Heaven knows what's ahead for you, it's a long-
range view! His presence is making way for you,
under and over ground! A fresh sound! Powerful
and true, you carry Heaven's sound; Miracles
abound!
You may feel like you're in captivity,
But love says, "I have won! It is done!"
My banner over you says, "IT IS DONE!"
"The power of breakthrough come!
You are blessed in Me;
I'm redeeming time,
Giving you fresh wine!"

THE MESSAGE REMAINS,
THE METHODS CHANGE

Out with the old; in with the new.
Culture and tradition shall not hold you!
The message remains, but the methods change!
Grass roots you're bursting through!
Pioneer, trail-blazer - the path before you is new!
Un-precedented breakthrough!
All things new; Heaven's breath upon you!
Unique start-ups; income streams of a Heavenly
kind
- You are a find!
The blueprints of Heaven are with you.
The message remains, but the methods change!

THE WEDDING AND THE
WINE

Lies like flies shall die!
Faithful and kind
Is removing evil arrows that come to blind.
The wedding and the wine;
Joy bells and presence that leaves no smoke.
You're not a joke!
Patience with self, hope!
Where you've lost hope in yourself
- Lost your fight for life,
You're invited to lay your efforts aside and feast.
You're not least;
You're not last - you shall go fast!
Words of condemnation shall go as you hand it over
and flow. The wedding is a celebration of all that's
fine;
You are the Bride.
Your Groom sees you perfect, ready and ripe!
His love has seized the day,
The canopy of hope surrounds you.
You are free to receive!
Mercy's kiss sees!

MESSY IS BEAUTIFUL

Green is a process, not a status!
You're not a cactus!
Not silenced; transparent and true
- Courage upon you!
Boots on the ground, you are found!
The best things are worth fighting for,
Your mess is a message and God says,
"You're my best!"

FAITH AND PATIENCE

Faith and patience inherit promises!
Covenant says, "I AM yours! I AM bread! I AM light.
I AM door, I AM Shepherd in the night!"
Deeper levels of trust are a must!
It's in I AM that you can step out!
You are true blue!
You shall follow and walk on through!
Faith, the supernatural force of God in and upon
you! Patience, your character!
I AM with you!

STAY IN YOUR LANE

Faithfulness wins the game!
He's making a way!
You're a conqueror!
One who habitually, continually, repeatedly
conquerors!
747 upon you all the way!
You're not flying solo!
Loved, appreciated, seen!
Robed, you are His queen!

Luke 7:47 TPT
"She has been forgiven of all her many sins. This is why she has
shown me such extravagant love. But those who assume they
have very little to be forgiven will love me very little."

FAITHFULNESS SEES

Intimidation, control, accusing voices are silenced!
His eye is on thee!
You are free!
"Tap into Me," says the King of Glory,
"I see!"
Rest amid the test!
Tap!
You're going to fly free!
What's in your hands?
The battle you face is won!
The internal war is done!
Faithfulness sees!
Step out willingly;
Where you are is not a co-incidence!
You are safely protected by the Canopy!
Faithfulness sees!

REST BRINGING YOU GODS
BEST

Your days are numbered;
Rest is bringing you God's best!
You have an advocate who speaks for you
when others oppose you!
The sin of unbelief has been dealt with!
Rise up, you people of power!
Not in the word's definition of power - God's power!
Shame, pain, your past - words spoken that had you
in a pin
No longer hold you in a spin!
God is elevating you!
"Come up higher, queen - it's time to dream!"
Humility is the seat you sit on!
Meek, not weak!
You're going to cut loose in this now time
and experience all God's created you to be!
Simply believe, you're worthy to receive!
Obedient in the ONE, it's finished in the SON!
Simply come!
The experience of rest is bringing you the best!

CROWNED AND
COMMISSIONED

Justice has heard!
You are not absurd!
The man acquainted with sorrow has faced your
tomorrow! Crowned, you carry a unique sound!
Found!
No longer rebound!
Pierced, poured out, he's bled!
You shall be fed!
No longer harking back; no longer hollow;
the crown of thorns replaced with a crown of
victory - removing the sting of sorrow!
Breaking through, you're coming through!
New territory; new alliances; fresh joy!
Clarity, confidence, courage are yours;
You are crowned, commissioned and carry Heaven's
sound!

VICTORY IS HEAVEN'S DECREE

Perspective shift!
Clarity!
The past has prepared you!
God has positioned you!
Promises are opening to you!
Open for promotion, "I've got you!"
Good things!
The ability to receive!
Mountains of doubt and cycles on repeat you shall
not see! Heaven wants you to receive!
Light as a feather amid all kinds of tether!
You're going to see clear and breathe fresh air!
There's been a clearing of the way, to make way!
Opportunities, divine connections, study;
New lands, new realms;
You haven't missed the boat;
You're anchored to HOPE!

SOAR ON HEAVEN'S ROAR

Bestowed you can go!
The Doe has released you to flow!
With eyes to see, you soar on heaven's roar!
You are a fragrant tree,
One who sows beautiful words and sets captives
free!
Amid the challenges; amid the difficulty!
Eyes for the King, the Doe has led you here to sow!
Beauty for ashes; widow with a mite
-Amid sacrificial, you'll see fire tonight!

THE HUSTLE

Hand it to Me and you shall go!
As you flow, the hustle will go!
"One in Me;
I've got you covered; can you see?
Strategy is found - and Me?
I give you light and easy!"
You say, "What's in it for me?"
I say, "I've got you covered.
Hand it over - I give you easy!
I've taken care of the struggle.
Hand Me your trouble!
Give it to Me and see what I see."
"I give you peace so you can face tomorrow.
Favour! Upgrade!
You're in My hand in the land!
I see!
I've faced your sorrow!
Hand it to Me.
You mean the world to Me.
I have faced your tomorrow!"

YOU'RE GOING TO FLY

You're going to see through eagle eyes and fly!
Trust a must amid the dust and rust!
Heaven's taking you higher, further;
You're going to reach the sky!
He's examined you with his golden eye!
His burden is easy; his yolk, light!
You are his great delight - one who has fresh insight!
What truth are you standing on?
That's all you need to examine!
He's passed the exam, the spotless Lamb!
Taking you higher, so you can fly above and not
below –
Where the weight is heavy and so is the load!
"Keep your eyes on Me!
Trust, rest, rely!
You're going to fly!"

NEW CEILINGS, NEW
FLOORS

The monkey shall no longer be on your back!
The areas that have been mocking you are now
serving you! The intimidation, fog and confusion is
lifting off of you!
The ceiling that's been over you is being lifted
and shall become your floor!
Expansion is knocking on your door!
Your heart shall once again soar!
You're going to see a sweet release
and relief from the monkey that's been harassing
you!
You're going to experience the courage
to pursue the good things the Father is calling you
to.
You're being released from oppression
and the dog of depression.
Evergreen surrounds you!
The enemy no longer makes a mockery of you!
New ceilings, new floors - good news!
It's time to nestle, amid the wrestle!

DREAMS ARE BURSTING TO LIFE

Breakthrough is upon you!
What feels like the end, is just the start!
It's always darkest just before dawn!
Let out that yawn, you're going to soar, fawn!
It's time to stand to your feet, step forward and see!
The emotional exhaustion,
Prolonged situations
and cycles of defeat
Shall no longer hold you in your street!
Fireball, you're going to dance on your feet!
Your dream hasn't died!
It's bursting to life!
Accept it!
Expect it!
Receive it!
Hope has a hold on you!
There's a maturing that's come forth in you;
You're resilient!
Your mess isn't going to take you out of God's best!
Come out from the cave;
Let out that WAR CRY.
It's time to arise!
Resurrected dreams are bursting to LIFE!

PROMISE OF PROMOTION

The foxes sent to destroy you –
Difficulty, distractions and opposition –
Shall disappear into thin air!
The promise of promotion is coming your way.
Lifting doubt,
You shall see the promise keeper meet you
as you lift up a victory shout!
The exhaustion and the foxes of indecision shall
disappear! You have the victory, dear!
The troubling foxes shall not spoil the vine!
Fresh perspective, fresh power,
Shall come upon you in this hour!
There's a tectonic shift in the ground;
Your roots let out Heaven's sound!
Promotion and favour shall be found!

REFRESHING RAIN IS HERE

You're going to see miraculous provision
and supernatural outcomes –
I see honeycomb and bees in the air!
It's pollination time!
You are ONE!
Unity is here!
One in the Son.
I see divine alignment, as provision has come!
Unity within you –
Letting go of old; walking into new.
Refreshing dew upon you.
In the test and in the mess,
He is faithful and true - always with you!
You came through your parents, not from your
parents; Heaven knows all about you
and loves you through and through!
There's a transfer taking place for you!
Receive it - refreshing rain is here;
It's overdue for you!!

MIRACLE TIME

You're going to inherit God's best for you!
In this new season that's upon you,
You're coming into all things new!
The head and not the tail –
The best is ahead for you!
God's giving you souls!
They're attached to your destiny, 2 by 2!
The Lion and the Lamb have faced your tomorrow!
The water that flows over you from the throne
is pure and light,
Giving you refreshing - and its full of life!
Stars shooting out of the mouth of the Lion
As heaven has the last laugh
Over your legacy, your life, your sparrow!
The awe and wonder of the majestic King
Leading you in His ring!
It's miracle time!
You are a miracle of love;
Treasured and chosen to reign on Earth
From Heaven above!

NO MORE STARK

I believe God is releasing fresh HOPE
into weary hearts in this hour.
He's dispelling darkness and bringing deliverance
where you've been at the end of your rope with
limited hope. I see you coming into the light of your
birthright!
Wrapped in His love, gentle as a dove,
You're going to feel His protection
and not feel sick in the stomach!
It's time to dive in deep with trust!
You're going to feel alive again!
You're going to trust!
You're going to see a release from the dust
and receive what you desire!
The promised child is coming!
God's going to give you hearts and descendants
As many as the stars in this season!
Your story is going to release many from gory!
You have been prepared,
For multitudes are coming into the Glory!
The games are going to stop!
You are marked!
One whose life shines in awe and wonder!
You haven't been forgotten, overlooked, or missed
out!
God sees and knows,
and the hope of glory is breaking you out!

HOLD THE LINE

It's a done deal, Heaven has won!
The psychological warfare shall not take you out on
the run! Hold the line, son!
Help is here, on the run!
Let out a shout of high praise,
VICTORY has come!
You've got this, son!
Believe, trust, stay in position –
Even through you're shaking;
As you praise, you're going to see a raise!
It's time to advance and take the head of the enemy!
No more tar, no more feather;
You're not a dirty duck,
You're an eagle who flies in the sky!
The Spirit of God reminds you,
"You're Mine, together we shall fly!"
You're not grounded
Even though it seems like you're surrounded!
Advancement is coming!
You shall not die; hold the line!

NEW SHOES

Heaven is upon you!
You're getting a revelation of his goodness that's
new! You're going to see God was carrying you!
The next leg of your journey,
You will see the dross and the difficulty removed!
The past no longer holding you,
You shall run fast!
He's giving you new shoes!
Hind feet!
The grit and the determination to follow through!
You're called and He's bringing you up and through!
You don't know how you're standing,
It's His presence sustaining you!
You've entered into a new era!
A new decade!
Depression is lifting!
Lack is not going to be on your back!
The God of more than enough is taking care of all
that stuff! You're not a victim of what happened to
you.
You're not a failure because of poor choices
Or zeal without enough wisdom!
What seems like a dead end, is just the start!
You've learned to lean
And that's the soft landing amid the dart!
Peace is your portion!
Peace with your past;
peace with the glass;

peace with the arrow that came to take you out in
the stark! You're not a target!
Peace has kept you amid the dart!
I see new beginnings, fresh shoots and grass roots!
Forgiveness is a gift to give yourself!
You've got the capacity to build,
And you're running with fresh shoes!
Grace has the last laugh!

TWO TREES

Heaven's paid the price!
It's a done deal!
You are free to come!
The old is dead; the new has come!
Positioned in the Son, you can come!
Posturing your heart to the ONE!
Come up higher, son - have fun!
Heaven's light as a feather;
There's ease on the run!
God is fully invested in YOU, son!
The Father and Son cut a covenant
that's never filing for divorce
or ending like a contract
Because of what you have or haven't done!
No more tree of good and evil!
The tree of LIFE says,
"Come! It's done, son! Just come!
Tap into Me and miracles you'll see."
You are worthy to receive! \
He bore it all, so you can have it all!
The new in you, the old is done!
Just come!
Deeper levels of trust.

Holy Spirit help is establishing you!
Truth has come!
The atmosphere of light and easy surrounds you,
son!
Just come.
Faithful and true is with you through life's dung.
He hung.
He's not in a rush;
He's often in the hush.
Just come.
With your humanity,
With your ashes, your dust –
Come.
The tree of LIFE has released you from strife;
He sees your willingness to trust!
Faith is activated;
Advancement is here!
You're going to live life in the fullness of the tree of
life,
No longer harking back to self-effort,
Your flocculating performance and a fading glory
that is a lie! You shall live life to the fullest and no
longer sigh!

ANOTHER OPPORTUNITY

It seems like tarry, but God says, "Carry!"
He's carrying the load, you shall not tarry!
There's a backlog of provision in the pipeline!
What seems like denial or delay is called,
'Miracle on the way!'
Miracles are God's specialty!
They're upon us every-single-day!
The heart of God is compassion!
He's moved by your situation,
And he's angered over the work of the Devil!
Jesus wept.
You're His true image!
You're going to see a divine exchange taking place
In the face of shame and disgrace!
What you're going through is another opportunity
to see:
I AM in your time and space!

NO MORE LOOSE CHANGE

There's a divine exchange taking place over your
situation! It's signed and it's sealed!
It's about to be delivered and it's real!
Upgrade, increase, and more is in store!
Hope Arise!
You're going to feel alive!
Healing is here!
Health is here!
Hope is here!
What the enemy meant for evil,
God is turning for good!
You have favour and honour before God.
The Bride has made herself ready,
Prepared to encounter her Groom!
Full of power,
Distractions of the world shall not rob you in this
hour!
The season has changed;
There's a divine exchange!
Double increase is being released;
Anointed and fresh power shall burst through you
in this hour! No longer blindsided and blinded by
the works of the enemy, The Bride shall feast and
celebrate
As the Groom has chosen you to be great!

WOUNDED AND WEARY

God is meeting you in the middle!
Where you've been wounded and weary amid teary,
The heart of God is helping you nestle.
You're going to see reprieve and healing from grief.
Supernatural rest is coming upon you so you can
settle.
From numb, to feeling again - you're not dumb, or a
bum; You're going to see miracles, Mum!
What matters to you, matters to God, too.
You're not petty or a sight to be sore,
Nor a bore;
What you've experienced has opened the door.
The heart of God is infusing you with more:
More strength, more sustaining power
And more desire to press through and soar!
You've got this and He's got you!
Wounded and weary, you're going to soar!

ALL THINGS NEW

Clean lenses, He's doing a new thing!
Can't embrace the new, with past experiences in
trauma informing you.
Suspicious and cautious no more!
One kiss from the King changes everything!
New alignments are yours!
New assignments, too!
God is bringing you out of the old,
As perfect love has made all things new!
It's time to start drinking and stop thinking!
No more cerebral, only the mind of Christ will do!
You're tapping into the truth
And connecting with the nature of God in you!
All things new!
The mind of Christ revealed through you!
New alignments, new assignments –
Only the best will do!
Mercy's kiss upon you!!

HE NAILED IT FOR YOU AND
FOR ME

Nailed to the tree, you were on His mind all the
time!
Trading sorrow, trading your tomorrow –
Release and reprieve!
He bore it all, so you can soar!
Your sin, your sickness, your depravity, haughty,
your filth –
He paid for it all, so you can be free from sore!
Failure, fraud no more!
Golgotha, the place of the skull;
The man acquainted with sorrow.
Fully God, fully man;
He was nailed, pierced and hung there for you and
for me!
A public spectacle to the powers and principalities;
An outrageous sign of love from above.
Perfect love.
Nailed.
Tortured.
Mocked.
Left for dead...
All for YOU, can you see?
Friend, you are FREE!
LOYAL LOVE
You are royalty;

You have destiny!
The role of monarchy is one who's anointed –
Not appointed, can you see?
You are commissioned to live as One, in the Son.
One who has the capacity to receive 'advise and guide'!
Loyal love has met you on the run!
The provision; the portion;
The presence of God is with you, son!
Your present is to be 'present in the present',
One with Loyal love!
Heaven's opened its womb,
Bringing fulfilment for you!
God be gracious to you, son, as you run!

NOT FORGOTTEN

Daughter,

You've always been on My mind!
I'm head over heels in love with you!
No matter the time that's gone by;
The decisions you've made that led you to sigh;
The times you thought, "Who cares? I'm on my own
anyway; This is my life!"

Daughter,

I've been with you through the strife.
You cried in the bottle,
Believing all you'd see from Me was throttle...
It's simply not true;
I gave it all for you.
I take the shame face off you;
The false version others gave you.
I care deeply for you –
Not what you think I need and want from you.
When you're ready, I'll be here;

I've not forgotten you.

Daddy

YOU ARE MY DELIGHT

You are My delight –
I've got you in My sight!
You're going to sigh with relief!
The road ahead is full of lean!
You shall see reprieve!
No longer tattered and scattered –
Or distracted.
Laser focus has come!
You're pregnant with promise!
Clarity is here!
Your debt has been paid and the path has been laid!
Fresh fire, fresh desire - fresh perspective, son.
I've wrestled over your blessing;
The power you need has come!
My delight, you shall see victory as you run!

VICTORY IS IN SIGHT

Heaven has seen;
Heaven has heard;
You're walking in power in his herd!
Victory is Heaven's decree;
Miracle breakthrough you shall see!
There's a truce over whose and who you are!
You are breaking through!
No more hiding in the night;
No more hark back out of sight;
You are victorious in God's light!
The Spirit of God draws you near,
Dispelling the lies that want to grip you in the air!
You're going to see reprieve! Retrieve!
New sound, new joy!
Victory is Heaven's decree over you;
Fear has to go!
Mercy kisses you shall know!

PIT TO PALACE

When you're helpless to save yourself, the Saviour
steps in! You may think your circumstance and
situation is a prison,
But the presence of God is with you!
Joseph lived thirteen years in captivity;
he was thirty when he took charge of Potiphar's
house.
For seven years, the people experienced bumper
crops!
God is with you and he'll pull out all the stops!
His seal of love set you apart from the start!
He's given you His bow,
The rainbow of colours;
His protective promise over you!
You are favoured;
You are his favourite!
Don't worry about the trouble!
God's giving you double!

ANCHORED TO HOPE

You're being re-aligned;
Faith has positioned you!
There's a re-directing taking place!
Heaven is pointing you back to your position and
path!
Not diluted, not divided;
You have one heart!
You feel like you've gone off track,
But the Spirit of God says,
"You're on track!
God is tracking with you!
You're in Him!
Anchored to hope, this boat shall stay afloat!

NOT GOING DOWN

"Give Me your YES and I'll give you the BEST!"
There's an invitation to COME - to step in, to
receive!
A standard called VICTORY has come!
Raised over your life, indeed delivery has come!
Breakthrough upon you!
The Sauls that have chased you down
No longer shall be found.
God's not double-minded about you,
He's all about you!
You're coming through this, not going down!

A PAUSE IS POWERFUL

In the waiting, you shall not want!
You've been given your hearts' desire;
You've experienced fresh fire!
Where plans haven't gone to plan,
God's love has you in his span!
He's never going to leave you abandoned in the
land!
The timeline of your life is full of fragrant oil!
Promise, provision, promotion is found
In His presence as you toil.

He's got this and He's got you!
Where you feel like you're walking in the unknown,
Know this: you are known!
God has not and will not abandon or forget you.
In the waiting, you shall not want!
In the waiting, you're gaining weight –
The kind of weight that knows how to slay the day!
The presence of God sustains you on the way!
The breath of God is bringing you seed –
What you need.
You're in good company in the wait;
Definitely not late!
Many of the greats had decades and generations to
wait...
You are not late.
Wait upon the Lord;
You are strong and you are courageous!
The wait is not in vain;
Actively press in as you wait!

A pause is powerful!

RAINBOW OF PROMISE

There's a rainbow of colours around you!
You're coming into all things new!
It's due!
The debt is paid!
The blood has followed through!
For you.
Courage and kind with you!
God calls you BRAVE;
You're not going to cave!
He's called you OUT –
To call you IN.
There's a fresh RING!
There's a signet
And it's got your name engraved on it –
Perfect and thin.
God's authority, seal and power
Upon you in this hour!
You're going to see the rainbow of promise
Settle you in the spin!

PIONEERS, YOU ARE DEAR

God is inviting you to take Him by the hand!
He's giving you new land!
Territory, destiny, souls!
Additional family!
The covenant Jesus cut with the Father has
positioned you!
He qualifies you, dear!
Pioneer, you are made of tough stuff,
One who has the ability to sacrifice
And press through hardship, dear!
You're anointed to breakthrough the headway, dear!

HEAVEN'S HONEY

Your greatest fear shall not keep you here!
The enemy has worked overdrive to keep you out!
You're a blessing –
One who has revelation knowledge in the house!
Expect good things to come!
The right alignments for you –
For God's life assignment for you –
To come!
God doesn't want you to take second best –
You're not dumb!
He wants you to eat the whole cookie,
Not just crumbs!
Heaven's honey, come!
Two by two you shall see the provision of God
In and released through you!

TRUST IS A MUST

The serenity prayer is yours!
Accepting the things you cannot change,
Changing the things you can,
Wisdom to know the difference!
For many of you, it's simply timing!
You're anointed for life and you're anointed for others!
When those two oils collide, you'll see unstoppable love!
Partnerships of trust!
Love, a must!
Sacrificial commitment!
The heart from the start and the desire to win hearts!
Trust is a must!
It's connected to your emotional life!
Satisfied in the now, content in not yet!
She's worth the wait; you won't be late!
Simply trust!

THE BEST IS YET TO COME

You're on track, target, time!
God's not taken by surprise!
You're going to dare to dream again- this week!
You're going to fly on eagles' wings!
No longer clipped!
No longer dipped!
Tared or feathered;
Feeling over and out, under the weather!
Heaven's riches;
Heaven's best!
You're released from disappointment!
Ready for divine appointments!
Destiny is here!
Oppressive situations shall fall;
You stand tall!
You have the strength of a mountain behind you!
Don't lose heart; I've got you
And I've seen this from the start!
You're not stalled; you're not stopped;
You're on time and you're going to be blown away
At the timing of God as he GIVES YOU THE BEST!

LOVE HAS WON

"Your destiny is found in Me", says the King of
Glory!
Jesus imparted the atmosphere of Heaven on Earth
So you could give birth!
Everlasting to everlasting,
His love is with you in the turf!
No longer turn or depart;
He's exchanged himself in your place –
You have a destiny that's come!
The wrap around presence has come!
Comfort, strength, stay;
With you all the way!
Confidence, clarity, glory;
Presence that's made way!
You have a destiny and it's here today!
In you, upon you, with you!
You've crossed the threshold from unknown
To known in the Son!
No longer undone!
No longer tied to lack –
It's behind your back!
Poverty gone!
No more harking back, depressed or condemned
Over what you have or haven't done!
It's been DONE so you can come!
Your time HAS come!
LOVE has WON!

ABOUT THE AUTHOR

Veronica is a voice of encouragement in the Christian faith community worldwide. She coaches students in identity and works with emerging writers seeing them launched in destiny!

www.veronicamcdonald.com.au.

As an author, Veronica is a prophetic style writer, words of life amid life's strife.

Genesis 3 is the heart of her message.

Ingram Content Group UK Ltd.
Milton Keynes UK
UKHW032238260423
420810UK00004BA/332